I0559502

Sorry To Hear About Your Turtle

By: Colleen Hollis

Illustrated and digitized by Colleen Hollis
Copyright © 2024 Colleen's Children Line Inc. Ltd.
Publisher: Colleen's Novels Inc. Ltd.
ISBN: 978-1-964768-00-7

I am so sorry to have hear about your beloved turtle

_____.

Most people have seen a turtle whether it is in the wild, at a zoo, or in a pet store.

However, most people will not be so lucky to get to call one their family.

Finish Line

Turtles may be known for being slow when it comes to their speed, but when it comes to racing right into our hearts, it took no time at all.

It truly is a special bond formed between a turtle and it's friend.

The love shared between you two has been sweet to witness.

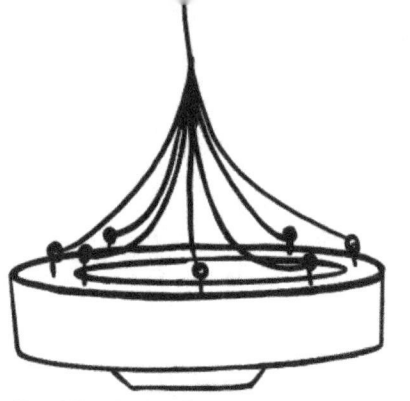

Wherever you were, there
your friend could always
be found too.

You have done such a great job being so responsible.

As you've learned, it's not just all playtime, there is daily effort required to care for a turtle.

No one can really understand
the love between a child and
their shelled friend, unless
they have had the pleasure
of taking care of one
themselves.

Not just anyone can comfort them in their time of need.

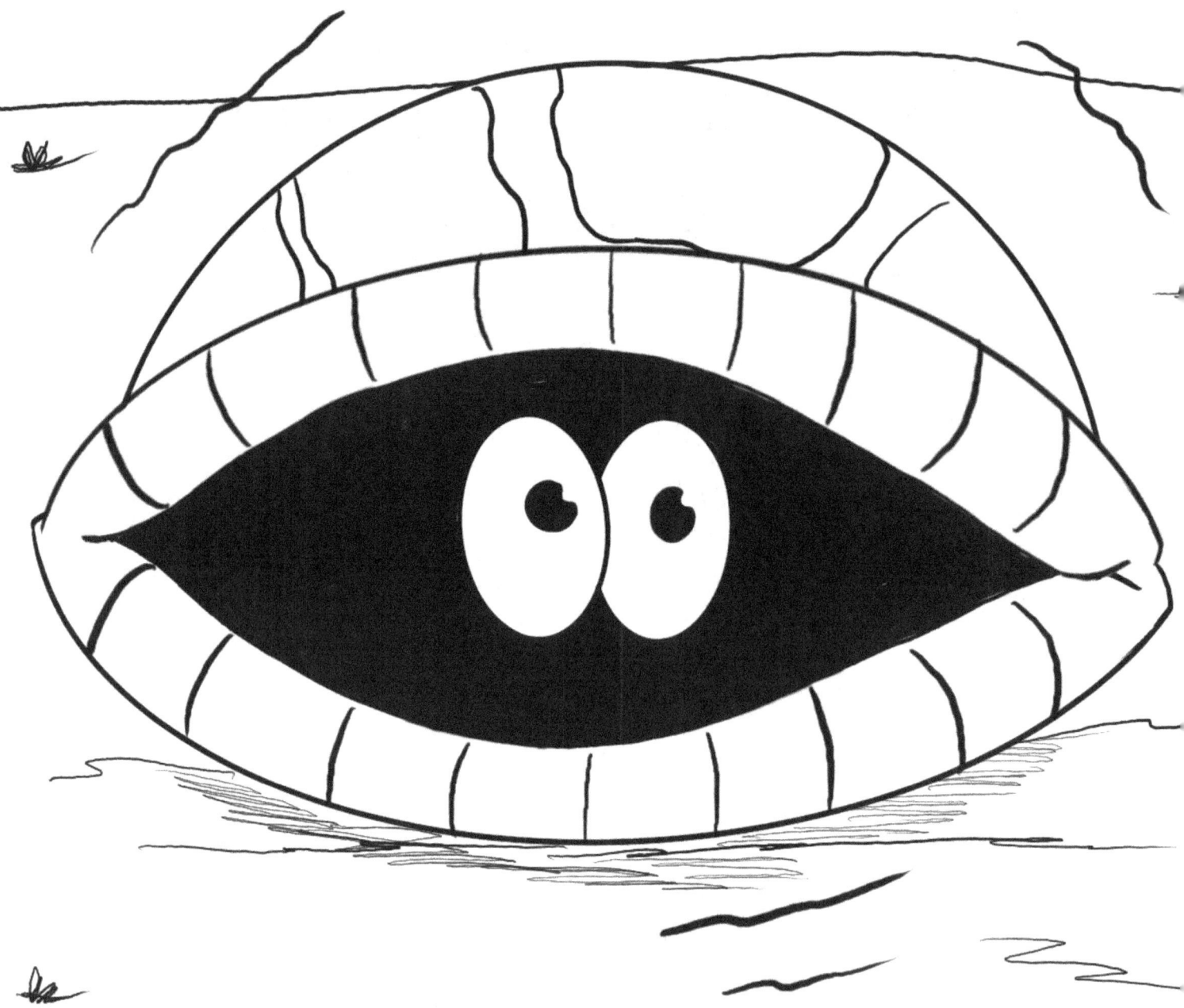

Day in and day out you did a great job being a turtle friend.

We understand this time may be sad, and that you may need a little more support than usual.

If you start to feel down and you need someone to listen, or give you a hug, know I am here for you.

You are never alone and can always safely express how you are feeling.

With time, you will be able to think back fondly on your turtle and smile, even if it doesn't feel that way now.

Try to focus on all the good times that you had playing together.

Reflecting on your adventures together will help with the healing process.

Friend's Facts

Friend's Name:_____

Friend's Age:_____

Friend's Favorite Food/s:_____
_____

Friend's Favorite Activity:_____
_____

Friend's Favorite Toy/s: _____
_____

Friend's Favorite Person/s:_____
_____

Feel free to write a little note, or share a memory or two.

Sorry To Hear About Your Turtle, is one of the books in the children's line from Colleen's Bereavement Line For Children. Colleen's Bereavement Line for Children is aimed to assist in the healing process of children that find themselves navigating the loss of a loved one or pet. Sorry To Hear About Your Turtle focuses specifically on those with a turtle friend.

A name can be added to the beginning of the book, while in the back of the book there is space to write memories about the shelled friend. Followed by a page for "Friend Facts" that can be filled in for a more personal feel.

All animal books in the series are interactive as well, they are in a coloring book format. Art has been shown as a useful tool that can aid in the healing process.